MW00940584

BEST OF ITALY
YOUR #1 ITINERARY PLANNER FOR WHAT TO SEE, DO, AND EAT

Wanderlust Pocket Guides

Copyright © 2015 Wanderlust Pocket Guides
Cover illustration © 2015 Wanderlust Pocket Guides Design Team

All Rights Reserved. No part of this publication may be reproduced, stored in a retrieval system, or transmitted in any form or by any means, electronic, mechanical, recording, or otherwise, without the prior written consent of the author.

Planning a trip to Italy?
Check out our other Wanderlust Pocket Travel Guides on Amazon:

BEST OF ROME: YOUR #1 ITINERARY PLANNER FOR WHAT TO SEE, DO, AND EAT

BEST OF VENICE: YOUR #1 ITINERARY PLANNER FOR WHAT TO SEE, DO, AND EAT

BEST OF FLORENCE AND TUSCANY: YOUR #1 ITINERARY PLANNER FOR WHAT TO SEE, DO, AND EAT

Also available:

BEST OF JAPAN: YOUR #1 ITINERARY PLANNER FOR WHAT TO SEE, DO, AND EAT

BEST OF TOKYO: YOUR #1 ITINERARY PLANNER FOR WHAT TO SEE, DO, AND EAT

BEST OF KYOTO: YOUR #1 ITINERARY PLANNER FOR WHAT TO SEE, DO, AND EAT

Our Free Gift to You

As purchasers of this paperback copy, we are offering you an **Amazon Matchbook download** of our colored **kindle version of this book for FREE.** Go to our book's page on Amazon and select the kindle version to download.

You **do not have to own a kindle** to read the kindle version of this book. Simply download the kindle reading app on your computer, tablet, or smartphone.

Florence

*"Italy, and the spring and first love all together should suffice
to make the gloomiest person happy."*

Bertrand Russell

Table of Contents

REGIONS OF ITALY

INTRODUCTION

Magnificent palaces since the beginning of recorded human history, rollicking coastline hugging shimmery azure sea, perfectly sculpted marble surpassing realistic beauty, acres of rich green vineyards binding under the weight of their dew-covered new grapes, and pieces art expertly executed to evoke emotions in you that you did not know were possible – Italy has it all. Yet the beauty of this ancient country is not only in its land or its art.

Visitors to the romantic county in every era have gushed about the flirtatious smile of a stranger on the street, or the glimpse of an expanse of tanned, bare leg just visible under the billowy folds of a skirt. This is a country that has insisted on existing in beauty long before the rest of the world had the luxury of worrying about anything more than subsistence, and this indulgent heritage shows, above all, in the evident pleasure its people still take in eating, walking, laughing, loving, or even "Il dolce far niente." – the sweetness of doing absolutely nothing. And it is this pleasure that Italians over the centuries have managed to distill onto blocks of marble, stacks of music sheets, stretches of canvas, bolts of fabric, and countless pristine white plates.

Luckily for visitors, Italians are not stingy with their joy in life. They delight in sharing with you their glorious Mediterranean sun, and everything that is underneath. Just laugh and be receptive, and you'll be sure to have the trip of a lifetime!

HOW TO USE THIS GUIDE

In this pocket guide of Italy, we outline first the top experiences you absolutely cannot miss, then other ones you'll want to check out, depending on your interests in food, wine, arts, history, and nature. There are also destinations for those preferring to be off the beaten path. All of these destinations are discussed in more detail in the third section of the book. Using these, you can customize your own itinerary!

For the first-time visitor, we have crafted an **itinerary** for **Rome**, **Florence**, and **Venice**, the three major cities to visit in Italy. For each city, we give you day-to-day recommendations for what you should see and eat, and include side trips if you have more time. In this way, you won't have to worry about missing any top attractions.

Then, in detail, we outline the cannot-miss spots in each major region in Italy, and all the fun things you could do. In northern

Italy, we discuss **Milan, Lake Como, Cinque Terres, Dolomites, Verona, Bologna, Venice**, and **Piedmont**. In central Italy, we talk about **Florence, Sienna, San Gimignano, Pisa, Montepulciano,** and of course, **Rome**, with a side trip to **Orvieto**. And finally, in the south, we tell you all about **Naples, Capri, Sorrento, Pompeii,** and the **Amalfi Coast**.

Finally, we give you more practical information on Italy, like whether you need a **visa**, the **best time to visit each region of the country**, **currency exchanges**, and **culture good-to-knows**. We also include **useful Italian phrases** at the end of this book. Armed with these, you'll have less to worry about, and more time to enjoy your trip!

Top Experiences in Italy

1. Step Back into History in Rome

Stand center stage at the Colosseum, and imagine looking up into the stands as a gladiator, your life about to be decided in a matter of minutes, or stroll in the Roman Forum, with your clients following you as you head into a Senate meeting. Rome is the real deal where history once took place.

Colosseum, Rome

2. Relive the Thriving Age of the Renaissance in Florence

In Florence, the cradle of the entire Renaissance period, you'll not have eyes enough to take in all the masterpieces by artists you've read about in your history textbooks. From Botticelli to Michelangelo, and of course, Leonardo da Vinci – the masters are all right here in Florence.

3. Celebrate Your Love in Venice

There is no place like Venice to make you feel the intoxication of love. Stroll hand in hand on cobble stoned streets, take a gondola ride while the sun sets behind you, or take a day trip to one of the islands in the area.

The Grand Canal, Venice

4. Hike along the Azure Path in Cinque Terre
Hike along the coast by the azure sea, and visit each of the five beautiful seaside villages collectively known as Cinque Terre. Smell the scent of the lemon groves, and stop to snap pictures with medieval churches.

5. Admire Lake Como, Where Nature and Architecture Unite
Lake Como region is renowned for its natural beauty decorated tastefully with exquisite lakeside villas. Not to mention all the water sports and hiking you could do here!

6. Eat, Eat, and Eat Some More!
We don't have to tell you Italian food is good. Just be sure to have all the best, most authentic food Italy has to offer while you are here. Hint: Neapolitan pizza in Naples, Florentine steak in Florence, and absolutely everything in Bologna!

7. Have Wine with Every Meal
Okay, maybe not with breakfast – but regions like Piedmont and Tuscany are some of the top win producers in the world. Visit vineyards if you have time, and drink directly from the source.

8. Drive Down the Amalfi Coast
Winding along the coast, you won't know which side to look – the shimmering Mediterranean seascape, or the colorful and stunning Amalfi architecture? Maybe your best option is to come from the sea on a boat!

9. Experience Style in Milan, the Fashion Capital of the World
Milan is home to some of the most elite brands in the world. But it is also home to great style – so if Prada is not in your budget, hunt down some affordable shopping in this very stylish city.

10. Un Cappuccino, Per Favore – A Cappuccino, Please!
Have a sip of Italian espresso, and you might understand why Italians turn up their noses at Starbucks. Know that Italians do not order cappuccinos and other milky forms of coffee after 11AM or meals – they believe drinking milky drinks on a full stomach really screws up your digestion.

11. La Dolce Vita!

Il dolce far niente – "the sweetness of doing nothing" is an art form the Italians have long learned to master. So when in Italy, do as the Italians do – celebrate life's pleasures, relax and let the sweetness of life sink in. Eat well, drink well, admire the beauty all around you, and enjoy!

Destination By Category

Food Lover – Bologna
Capital of the Emilia-Romagna region – which is known to have the best food in Italy – Bologna is recognized as the gustatory heaven of the country. Definitely try the freshly made pasta, cured pork, and cheese from the surrounding region. Actually, just try it all!

Wine Lover – Piedmont and Tuscany
Piedmont and Tuscany are the most famous wine-producing regions in Italy. Piedmont is known for red wines, such as Barbera, Nebbiolo, and Dolcetto, as well as its more famous white wines including Moscato and Cortese. Tuscany produces Chianti, Brunello, Vin Santo, and Vino Nobile. In either region, there will be plenty of vineyards and wineries for you to tour, and at the end of each tour, drink!

Tuscany

Art Lover – Florence

Florence was the cradle and heart and soul of the Renaissance art scene, where masters like Michelangelo and Leonardo da Vinci lived and made their art. This beautiful city that once inspired the world's greatest art is now home to some of the best galleries in the world, displaying the works of those of its most famous residents.

History Lover – Rome and Pompeii

Rome and Pompeii were both once where history actually took place. In Rome, you'll find the epicenter of the Roman Empire, and get to visit the Colosseum, Forum, and many other Roman structures. Pompeii is also a must, as volcanic ashes from Mt. Vesuvius preserved many facets of daily life in ancient Rome.

Nature Lover – Lake Como, Dolomites, Amalfi Coast, and Capri

Located on the Mediterranean, Italy has no shortage of scenic spots. You can take a boat ride along Lake Como, ski or hike near the Dolomites, or visit the beautiful coastal Amalfi or the island of Capri. Go ahead, dive into that stunning azure water!

Italy Off the Beaten Path

To snap a picture with your sweetie in the same balcony that Shakespeare's most famous lovers, Romeo and Juliet, once occupied, visit charming **Verona**. For an authentic local experience, visit **Siena** in Tuscany for its famous horse race, Il Palio, in which the locals take great pride and stake much personal allegiance. For medieval architecture ensconced in attractive hills, visit **San Gimignano** or **Orvieto**. **Montepulciano** is also great, and produces good wine. For some hiking next to the coast, amid rustic villages, visit the five towns collectively known as Cinque Terre. To experience the Amalfi Coast, visit **Sorrento** or **Positano**.

Verona

Best of Italy Itinerary – Rome, Florence, and Venice

Rome, Florence, and Venice are likely the three must visit cities for first-time visitors to Italy. They will allow you to enjoy the many attractions Italy has to offer, from nature to history, from art to outdoor activities.

Getting In and Getting Between the Cities

You should either do Rome, Florence, and Venice in that order, or the reverse works too. However, Rome is more accessible by air than either Florence or Venice.

If coming into Rome, depending on where you are traveling from, you'll either fly into the Ciampino Airport, or Leonardo da Vinci International Airport, both near Rome. There is a direct bus that runs from da Vinci Airport to the central train station, known as "Termini Station" in central Rome.

From Rome, you can travel to Florence on a speed train in two hours. The main station in Florence, very centrally located, is Firenze Santa Maria Novella.

Venice is served by Marco Polo Airport, located on the mainland. To get to the lagoon where all attractions are, you'll need to take a waterbus, a pricey water taxi ($100+), or a bus that takes you to Piazzale Roma, the main bus station on the Venice Lagoon. Alternatively, you can take the train directly to Venezia Santa Lucia train station, which stops at the lagoon.

In general, staying near the train stations will save you time and make it easier to take a day trip somewhere. Also, most train stations have shuttles (or water buses in Venice) that take you to and from the airport.

Rome

Recommended Stay: 3 to 6 Days
Avoid mid-July through August because it'll be very crowded, hot and very humid. Tourist season and the heat wanes in mid-late September.

Day 1

Spend a day walking around the ancient Rome, buy a combo ticket for the Roman Forum and Colosseum (tip: line is shorter at the Forum) and bypass the general line.

Day 2
Visit the Pantheon, Trevi Fountain, Piazza di Spagna and Spanish Steps, and Piazza Venezia.

Day 3
Visit the Vatican City and St. Peter's Basilica. Book your lines online beforehand because the line always wraps around corners. Expect crowds of sweaty people.

Day 4
Visit Trastevere, relax and eat at various romantic restaurants with cute outdoor seating, take a stroll in Trastevere afterwards. Shop at Via del Corso.

Side Trips:
Take a Day Trip to visit the ruins of Pompeii.
Take a Day Trip to ancient hill town Orvieto.
Take a Day Trip to Naples.

Florence

Recommended Stay: 2 to 3 Days

Day 1
Visit the Duomo in the morning, have lunch at Mercato Centrale. In the afternoon, visit the Piazza della Signoria, and the adjacent Palazzo Vecchio, before heading to the nearby Uffizi Gallery after 4pm, to avoid long lines. Have dinner nearby and there's usually wonderful live music at night in the Piazza della Signoria outside.

Day 2

If you're an art fan, visit the Accademia for more Renaissance masterpieces, including Michelangelo's David. Head to Ponte Vecchio, explore the shops on it. Then, visit the Pitti Palace or Boboli Gardens. Admire the panoramic view of Florence at Piazzale Michelangelo at sunset.

Day 3
Tuscany towns are beautiful and tasteful (more than just good wine). We highly recommend a day trip to Siena.

Side Trips:
Pisa
Siena
San Gimignano or Montepulciano (both are hill towns)

Venice

Recommended Stay: 1 to 2 Days

Day 1
Visit the Basilica San Marco (St. Mark's Basilica) and adjacent square. Admire its beautiful Byzantine architecture. Visit the adjacent Palazzo Ducale (Doge's Palace). This plaza is often very crowded so we recommend heading there first thing in the morning to avoid crowds.

Head to Rialto Market and the Rialto Bridge. Have lunch nearby while enjoying the beautiful view of the Grand Canal. Try cicchetti with a glass of white wine at a cicchetteria - Italian small plates.

Take a gondola or water bus ride along the grand canal. Explore either Dorsoduro sestiere (district) or Cannaregio sestiere. Both of these are less packed with tourists and equally beautiful. Enjoy dinner on either Cannaregio or Dorsoduro, where you'll find friendlier prices and more authentic food than restaurants near San Marco or San Polo.

Day 2

Get lost! Literally, wander the streets of Venice and explore a different sestiere from your first day here. Fans may want to see the Peggy Guggenheim Museum or Ca'd'Oro. Then, take a day trip to nearby Isle Murano or Burano.

Side Trip:
Murano or Burano (half day)
Verona

DESTINATIONS (BY REGION)

NORTHERN ITALY

MILAN

Milan, in northern Italy, is the most modern, fashionable, and cosmopolitan city of the country. Partially destroyed by bomb raids during World War II, the city has managed to rebuild itself into a modern metropolis at the center of the Italian economy. Compared to other tourist destinations in Italy, Milan is rather more renowned for its worldly pleasures – of the current century – shopping, football, opera, and nightlife. This modern penchant is clearest when every spring and autumn, fashion aficionados and supermodels descend from around the globe for Milan's fashion weeks.

But Milan is nonetheless a city with over 2,600 years of history, as evidenced by sites like the Duomo, one of the grandest Gothic cathedrals in the world, the Castello Sforzesco, a grand medieval castle, or Santa Maria delle Grazie Basilica, which contains of course, Leonardo da Vinci's world famous mural, The Last Supper. In fact, the churches in Milan predate their counterparts in Rome, as Milan was the capital of the northern part of the late Roman Empire.

Milan Duomo

Sights

Duomo (Milan Cathedral)

The main cathedral of the city, the Duomo with its white marble façade, and hundreds of spires and thousands of statues, was first constructed in 1386. The cathedral houses some of the most magnificent treasures you'll see in Milan, but for an unforgettable experience, climb the 250 steps (or take a lift for €5) to the roof, and enjoy a spectacular view of the city, and on a fine day, of the snow-capped Alps in the distance. You can also admire 3,600 statues and 135 spires, carved from pink Candoglia marble.

Duomo Square

Piazza del Duomo is the grandest square in the city, and its cultural and social heart with several of Milan's most famous sights. Aside from its namesake cathedral, and the classy Galleria shopping mall, you can also find the Royal Palace, an 18th century building that has been converted to an art exhibition hall, and several other austere old buildings. The street that leads to the square is lined with huge lights, huge buildings, and an enormous statue of King Victor. It also has many lovely cafes where you can sit and watch the beautiful people of Milan, who visit the area of its top-quality restaurants and shops.

Saint Maurice Church
This stunningly frescoed Renaissance church is considered the "Sixteen Chapel" of Milan. Most of the paintings on the church's ceilings are the works of Bernardino Luini.

Saint Mary of the Graces (Chiesa di Santa Maria delle Grazie)
This UNESCO World Heritage basilica is one of the masterpieces of the Renaissance architect Donato Bramante. Its delicately carved exterior supports the magnificent dome, while the interior boasts a whimsical atmosphere filled with light.

The Last Supper, Leonardo da Vinci's masterpiece, is housed in the rectory separate from the main structure. While this world famous fresco is now 100% restoration, it remains da Vinci's most influential work artistically, and one of the city's treasures. Due to its popularity, it is best to reserve tickets a few months before your visit at the official website: http://www.cenacolovinciano.org/sito/home.html.

Galleria Vittorio Emanuele II
World's top fashion brands, like Louis Vuitton and Prada, all have boutiques in this splendid 19th century palace turned mall with its stunning mosaic floor, wondrous glass roof and cupola. There are also tons of upscale eateries, art galleries, and bookstores. At Christmas time, it becomes an especially enchanting place with lights and themed decorations.

Saint Ambrose (Basilica di Sant'Ambrogio)
Entrance is free to this Lombard Romanesque style basilica located on the Piazza San Ambrogio. Originally built between 1080 and 1140, the basilica is constructed with technical

innovations like the groined cross vault and wider vaulted naves ahead of its time, and is today second only to the Duomo in Milan in terms of renown. There are also many artistic masterpieces inside, like the Vuolvinious golden alter, a Carolingian goldsmith masterpiece, and the very important fourth century mosaics of the chapel of San Vittore in Ciel d'oro. The magnificent marble pulpit itself dates back to the 10th century.

Villa Necchi Campiglio
Visit this beautiful villa, which was built in the 1930's and once belonged to the Necchi Campiglio industrial family, for a great collection of artworks, including Sironi, Martini, and de Chirico, as well as many 18th century decorative art pieces.

Castello Sforzesco
This iconic red brick castle once belonged to the powerful clans of the Sforza-Visconti, who ruled over Renaissance Milan. The castle's history is made up of famous figures - its defenses were designed by da Vinci himself, who counted the Sforzas among his best patrons, and later, Napolean drained the moat, and removed the drawbridges. Today, it is host to seven specialized museums, exhibiting many intriguing fragments of Milan's history, including the final work of Michelangelo, the Rondanini Pietà.

La Scala Opera Theater (Teatro alla Scala)
One of the most renowned opera houses in the world, La Scala has seen performances by world-class stars like Maria Calla and Pavarotti. Aside from the program, the theater's rich interior, decorated with magnificent chandeliers and staircases, will be memorable on its own. If you'd like to attend an opera, be sure to book tickets well in advance. Owing to its fame, tickets at the La Scala can be quite pricy.

Brera Art Gallery (Pinacoteca di Brera)
One of the most important museums in the world in the ranks of the Louvre or El Prado, Brera is home to some of Italy's most iconic masterpieces, such as "the Kiss" by Francesco Hayez, the

"Lamentation of Christ" by Mantegna, the "Supper at Emmaus" by Caravaggio or the "Marriage of the Virgin" by Raphael.

Monumental Cemetery (Cimitero Monumentale)
These 250,000 square meters are no ordinary cemetery, but rather the largest Art Nouveau museum in the world. Milan's old burial grounds are decorated with lavish sculptures, impressive mausoleums and monuments. The focal point of the whole complex is the "Temple of Fame", where celebrated Milanese, including Luca Beltrami, Arturo Tscanini, Salvatore Quasimodo, Giogio Gaber, and Alessandro Manzoni, are buried.

Experiences

Soccer/ Football
Italians live and breathe soccer. Watch AC Milan or FC Internazionale at the famous Giuseppe Meazza Stadium, also known as San Siro, which is home stadium to both clubs. Tickets are available in advance or on the day of the match. As many as 60 matches are played per year from late August to late May here, be sure to catch one!

Shopping
To shop for top brands, many of which are Italian, head to the so called Fashion Quadrangle, a set of neoclassical blocks roughly between Duomo Square, Cavour Square, and San Bahila Square.

For more affordable shopping, head to Vercelli Avenue, or Buenos Aires Avenue, which is reputedly the longest shopping street in Europe.

Eat and Drink

Traditional Milanese cuisine is hearty and filling, including osso buco (braised veal shanks), risotto alla Milanese (chicken broth risotto made with saffron), and cotoletta alla Milanese, a thick, crispy fried veal cutlet. You can sample these authentic dishes at informal, often family-run trattorie and osterie.

Milanese tend to dine earlier than Romans or Florentines, with lunch served between 12:30PM to 2:30PM, and dinner between 7:30PM and 9:30PM. Both meals are often preceded by the "apertivo", which is Milan's version of the happy hour. However, this is an occasion to socialize rather than to get drunk, as Italians are actually very moderate drinkers.

From 7PM to 9PM, you'll find many bars offering drinks and cocktails at a fixed price (€5-8 each), accompanied by free all-you-can-eat buffets with snacks, pastas and many other small dishes. Note that this is not a "free dinner", as Italians will immediately consider you tacky if you try to fill up on finger food for dinner. Think about it as an appetizer to be enjoyed with a drink, before you head out for dinner properly.

Nightlife

Milan has a flourishing nightlife that you can enjoy. Start with Avenue Como, near Garibaldi Station, which is full of bars and high-end clubs. In the summertime, you'll find all of Milan's most attractive people here.

Another place to enjoy nightlife is Navigli quarter, near Porta Ticinese Avenue and XXIV Maggio Square, where there are lots of small pubs, outdoor cafes and restaurants right by the canal.

LAKE COMO

A popular resort destination since Roman times, Lago di Como, as Lake Como is known in Italian, includes the tranquil lake and its picturesque surroundings. Its inverted "Y" shape gives Como an extended shoreline, enclosed by mountains and hills, dotted with the occasional villa from millennia past. Aside from lounging on the beach, you can explore lovely lakeside towns such as Bellagio, Varenna, and Menaggio, or go hiking, take boat trips, or partake in a variety of water activities.

Try to avoid visiting on the weekends, as you'll have to jostle with hassled Milanese escaping from the nearby city. July and August, as in most destinations in Europe, are the most crowded months.

Sights

Varenna

As the ferryboat approaches this little fishing village on the eastern shores of Lake Como, you are transported to a whole other world, with its stunning narrow alleyways and winding streets you'll enjoy getting lost in, rows of narrow, colorful houses, and a small beach lined with many boats, all overlooked by the charming Castle Vezio. Explore the town on foot, and be sure to sample some delicious fresh fish in one of the local trattorias. After lunch, hike up to the castle for great views of the lake.

Bellagio
Located at the beautiful junction where the three branches of Lake Como come together, Bellagio is known as the pearl of the lake region and its most famous tourist destination. Its unique setting offers breathtaking views you cannot find elsewhere. Explore the town's cobblestone streets, and step into alleyways that take you back into its historical past. Due to its popularity, Bellagio is also more expensive than the other towns on the lake, but for a first-time visit, you simply cannot miss this gem.

Menaggio
Leaning at the foot of the mountains, Menaggio offers an incomparable setting for a myriad of outdoor activities like hiking, swimming, windsurfing, and rock climbing. The lakeside promenade looks straight out of a fairy tale with its ornate villas, against the backdrop of Bellagio and Varenna hazy in the distance. History buffs can walk to the upper part of the town, where the remains of medieval ruins with the original castle walls have been well-preserved and open to public view.

Como
With a good historic center and lively squares dotted with cafes where you'll want to linger, Como is a good "home base" for your time in the lake region. There are several walking paths near town, or you could take the funicular to the nearby village of Brunate, soaring 720 meters above Como, for its hiking trails and beautiful views of the lake and the Alps.
Villas

Resorts and villas have been built in the area since Roman times, when Pliny the Younger built the Comedia and the Tragedia. While these are no longer standing, there are still many villas worth visiting for their admirable gardens and historical architecture on the shore of Lake Como. Villa Balblanello and Villa Carlotta are both great options.

Experiences

Boat Trip
Be sure to take at least one boat ride while you are in Lake Como. Most of the popular tourist towns like Bellagio and Varenna can be easily accessed by water. You won't forget the view of the approaching shoreline!

Funicular
These hillside trolleys bring you to the top of the hills surrounding Lake Como. Villages like Brunate offer stunning views of the whole area.

Water Sports
There are many vendors for water sports on the shore of the lake.

Hike in the Mountains
Many routes that take you high into the mountains start from lakeside towns you would have visited – like Menaggio or Dongo. From some viewing spots, it is possible to see both Lake Como, and the nearby Lake Lugana. Visit a tourist center in a town to ask about the best options.

CINQUE TERRES AND NEARBY RIVIERA TOWNS

Literally "Five Lands", Cinque Terres refers to a rugged stretch of the coast of the Italian Riviera in the Liquria region of Italy, to the west of the city La Spezia. This collection of small coastal villages – Riomaggiore, Manarola, Corniglia, Vernazza, and Monterosso – is on the UNESCO World Heritage for stunning vistas and old-world charm. Mediterranean herbs and trees grow from the top of the hills all the way down the slopes to the water in each, decorated here and there by thousands of years of human activity, most notably rustic wine terraces where you can still sample the famous dry white that the region has been producing for as long as it has been inhabited.

Trains from La Spezia, Milan, Rome and other cities in Italy take you away from the bustling city life to this region, where you can enjoy a few days of the expansive Italian seascape. A walking trail, known as "Sentiero Azzurro" (Azure Trail) connects these five gems together. As its name implies, the walk is as beautiful as the villages themselves.

Note that with the exception of Monterosso, all of the towns rise steeply from the sea, which can be challenging to navigate if you are toting a large suitcase. Also, while the local train stops at each town, the main line connecting to the rest of Italy only stops at Monterosso, so you may need to transfer if you plan to get around by train.

Corniglia

Sights

Riomaggiore
The southern-most of the cluster, Riomaggiore is watched over by an ancient stone castello that is so old that when a document from the 6th century already describes it as "ancient". Quadrangular walls surround the structure with two circular towers built to guard the town from naval attacks. It has since been converted into a cemetery, and today stands as one of the monuments of the Parco Nzionale delle Cinque Terre.

The town is as charming today as it must have been in the past, where during the day you can hear bell towers chiming, and at night frenetic chatters from the frogs as fishing boats take off from the shore for night fishing – as the inhabitants of the village have done for thousands of years. You can find many cafes, bars, restaurants, and gelateria along the town's main street, Via Colombo, as well as many small shops selling fresh fruit, Italian sausages, cheeses and olives. Pick up a yummy picnic before you head to the beach, or into the hills for a hike.

Manarola

Stairs, lined by ancient trees, run from the top of the hills all the way down to sea level in Manarola. Half way down, you'll find a charming little terrace with picnic tables, where you can join locals having a simple lunch. Further down, large rocks cluster on the coast, next to which is a small pier where you can wade out into the azure Mediterranean water, without too many people around. Like other towns, you can find plenty of lovely, locally-owned places to eat and drink here.

Corniglia

Smaller and quieter than the other villages, Corniglia sits 300 feet above the Ligurian Sea, the only one of the five towns that is not near sea-level. The path to the town is lined with lemon trees, vines, lilies and other vegetation, lending the air here a fresh perfume that no chemicals can replicate.

As the town is on top of a hill, it is only reachable by climbing the 365 steps – one for each day of the year – or take the bus that runs between 7am to 8pm daily, or 8am to 8pm on weekends, that departs from the train station.

Vernazza

Take the Azure Trail from the olive grove above Corniglia north, with great views backward toward both Corniglia and Manarola, passing by the tiny hamlet of Prevo, and the famous Guvano Beach, and you will soon come upon Vernazza. You will first see the two ancient towers before finding the town proper. At first sight, Vernazza is a bit rundown, with the paint on some buildings peeling off, but don't let that fool you. There is a lively and boisterous scene here, especially at night. Take a walk along the strip of beach and take in the mountainous coastline hiding the next town of Monterosso, or have wine at the many outdoor cafes on the main street.

Monterosso

Monterosso contains an old town, and a new town that was developed from the 1950s onward. The older part is similar to other Cinque Terres towns, with a number of boutiques and other shops. The new town has a nice sandy beach with lots of umbrellas, restaurants and cafes seaside. Don't miss the large statue at the end of the beach, holding out a terrace!.

Experiences

Coastline Hiking
Cinque Terre offers some of the most scenic coastline hiking trails in the world. Aside from the Azure Trail, which requires a pass, there are a number of other options that do not require a pass, and are just as beautiful.

The path from Riomaggiore to Manarola is called Via Dell'Amore (Love Walk). This is a paved path that is easy to walk for people of most age and physical condition.

From Manarola to Corniglia, there are two paths – one closer to the water and easy, which takes about 30 minutes, the other further uphill. Manarola also has its own vineyard path that is quite beautiful.

From Corniglia to Vernazza, there is a path through uneven terrain that takes about 2 hours, this can be a bit more challenging than the others.

The trail from Vernazza to Monterosso is the steepest with 250 meters of climbing over uneven rocks, making up 750 steps all together. The path winds through gorgeous olive orchards and vineyards, and offers dramatic ocean views, but do be careful, as there is a real danger of falling 12 to 15 feet if you lose your balance.

Swimming

Each town offers opportunities for swimming in the ocean. The largest sandy beaches can be found at Monterosso, while there is a smaller one at Vernazza, and pebble beaches near Riomaggiore and Corniglia. From Manarola and Riomaggiore, you can dive off of rocks, as the sea becomes deep rather quickly. These are also the quietest swimming spots, since the harbors are the bottom of long descending paths.

Eat and Drink

Fresh catches from the sea unsurprisingly dominate the local cuisine at Cinque Terre. Anchovies, stuffed with a breadcrumb based filling then fried, are a must-try local specialty. Stewed cuttlefish, stuffed calamari, and spiced octopus, are also fresh and delicious here.

Other regional favorites include farinata, a savory and crunch pancake made of chick pea flour, and trofie, a pasta made from chestnut or wheat flour that is an ancestor of the modern pastas. Egg frittata is a popular antipasto, while vegetable pies called "torte di verdura", prepared with a stuffing of local wild herbs and vegetables combined with egg and ricotta cheese, are frequently ordered from bakeries and pizzerias. Corniglia is famous for miele di Corniglia, gelato made with local honey.

The fame of Cinque Terre is largely due to its two most popular products – a dry white wine simply called "Cinque Terre", and a dessert wine called "Sciacchetrà" made by distilling prime grapes to the point of holding only a few drops of sweet juice. So be sure to try both with your meals here.

The region is also known for its lush lemon trees. An annual Lemon Festival is held in Monterosso each year during the season of the Pentacost. Steeping lemon peels in pure alcohol and adding sugar and water makes, Lemoncello, another popular dessert wine.

DOLOMITES (ITALIAN ALPS)

The Dolomites, located in northeastern Italy, is a strange collection of Alpine pinnacles that shoot straight up like chimneys, which you can see in the background of Leonardo da Vinci's Mona Lisa. Between mountain peaks, rivers meander through lush valleys dotted by quaint villages, and pristine lakes overlooked by castles straight out of fairy tales.

The area was declared an UNESCO World Heritage Site for its rich Austrian history that remains mostly undisturbed by modernity. Most local residents are bilingual German and Italian speakers who eat yogurt for breakfast, and can still yodel as well as their counterparts on the other side of the border in Austria.

Lake Caress, Dolomites

Sights

Cortina d'Ampezzo

Situated in the middle of the Ampezzana Valley and surrounded on all sides by the Dolomites, Cortina d'Ampezzo is a village that offers a spectacular vista no matter where you are standing. As such, the town is popular with the jet-set crowd both in summer and winter, for hiking, mountain climbing, and skiing. You can also participate in base jumping, paragliding, and hang gliding.

VERONA

Situated an hour away from Venice in Italy's Veneto region, Verona earned its fame as the setting of Shakespeare's most famous star-crossed lovers – Romeo and Juliet – met their heart-wrenching end. Less touristy and crowded than Venice, Verona offers a more relaxed atmosphere where you can wander in peace.

The city dates back more than two thousand years. In the first century AD, it came under Roman rule, the evidence of which can still be seen in many ruins, most notably the Arena, which looks like a copy of Rome's Colosseum. There are also evidence of Austrian occupation in the 12th to 14th centuries, when the powerful Scaligery family ruled over Verona, in the city's fortifications and the family emblem, a ladder, on architectures across the city.

Sights

The Arena
This enormous Roman amphitheater is crumbling on the outside, but still retains its elliptical shape erected in the first century AD. It is the world's third-largest amphitheater to survive from antiquity, though much of its outer ring was damaged during an earthquake in 1117. You can still catch an opera performance here today during the summer season.

Piazza delle Erbe
The piazza served as the Roman forum in ancient times, and is still a focal point of the city today. On the square you can find the "Britney Verona" fountain, the 14th century Gardello Tower, and a market that is, admittedly, rather touristy.

Basilica of St. Zeno (Basilica di San Zeno Maggiore)
Located slightly off city center, this basilica is rich in devotional artwork and historical preservation. The church is dedicated to

fourth century North African priest Zeno, who was ordained Bishop of the city in 363, and has become the city's patron saint after his death. The body of Zeno lies in the church's undercroft, with a Medieval statue of the saint watching over the grounds in full episcopal robes, dangling a golden fish at the end of a fishing rod, paying homage to his humble start in life.

Juliet's House (Casa di Guilietta)
Here is reputedly where Shakespeare's lovely heroine leaned from the balcony, speaking with her lover below. The house is especially popular with love-struck teenagers who take photos in a similar position as Romeo and Juliet.

In reality, the house has no connection with the Bard's fictional characters, though it is indeed an old structure. The city added the balcony in 1936, and declared the house Juliet's to attract tourists. More discerning visitors can still enjoy a small collection of Renaissance frescos.

Juliet's Balcony

Castelvecchio
This 14-century castle is currently an art museum that is packed with medieval sculpture and Renaissance paintings. Children enjoy running around castle fortifications and the extensive ramparts, while the parents can look over from the adjoining bridge for some fantastic views of the castle on the river.

Experiences

Sweeping Views
The best view of the city can be had from the top of Castel San Pietro, which towers over the rooftops that glimmer under the sun.

Shopping at Verona's Golden Mile
Via Mazzini, between Piazza Bra and Piazza delle Erbe, is known as Verona's Golden Mile, where you can find most of the major Italian labels. If you are not prepared to drop the big bucks, it can still be fun to window shop and people watch.

Eat

Verona boasts of a strange local delicacy – horsemeat. Try Pastissada de caval, an ancient horsemeat stew that is tender and flavorful with a myriad of herbs and vegetable, served with polenta. For those not keen on eating horses, Brasato all'Amarone is a braised beef dish cooked with Amarone wine, also served with polenta.

Veronese "bollito misto" is also very good. This mixed meat dish popular across northern Italy, known as "lesso" here, is topped with a special sauce – made from meat stock, grated stale bread, ox marrow, and abundant black pepper – only found here in the city. It is traditionally served at Christmas time, but now can be found year round.

VENICE AND SURROUNDING TOWNS

There is simply no place like Venice. This sanctuary on a lagoon is as lovely as it was six hundred years ago despite heavy tourism – 56,000 residents and 20 million tourists per year – and has retained its romantic charm. Once called the Most Serene Republic of Venice, Venice dates back to 827 AD, and has prospered through the century as an Italian city state under the rule of a Roman-style Senate, headed by the Doge.

All together, the area known as Venice comprises of 118 islands arranged in districts known as "sestieri". Most of your sightseeing will be in the sestieri of Cannaregio, Castello, Dorsoduro, San Polo, Santa Croce, and San Marco. There are no cars here, as the city is easily walkable. Strolling, you can get from one side of Venice to the other in a matter of hours. There are also vaporetti (water buses) and water taxis that can get you from one part of the lagoon to another. And of course, within the main tourist districts, you'll have the opportunity to take a gondola ride, quite romantic, even if it does not get you to your destination in a hurry.

Venetian Canals

Sights

Saint Mark's Basilica (Basilica di San Marco)
Located on the Piazza San Marco, Saint Mark's Basilica is one of Venice's top attractions. This impressively stunning building is renowned worldwide for its large collection of priceless artifacts, and a seemingly endless supply of secret places with a storied past. Do not miss the symbol of the basilica – the Greek Hellenistic sculpture, the gilded bronze horses.

As with most churches in Italy, you should dress appropriately to gain entrance. No short skirts or bare shoulders allowed, and the same applies to large backs or rucksacks (you'll have to deposit them around the corner from the main entrance.

Doge's Palace (Palazzo Ducale)

This beautiful palace once served as the residence for Venice's doges, who were the supreme authority of the former Republic. It is adorned by art throughout, designed to display the wealth and power of the rulers of Venice.

You can get regular tickets either at the Palace, or across the square at the Museo Correr. But consider joining the Secret Itinerary guided tour for €20, which lets you discover secret parts of the palace where the city's administration held office, as well as Casanova's jail and the five hundred year old roof structure.

Bell Tower of St. Mark (Campanile di San Marco)
Climb to the top of the tower for great views of Venice and the lagoon. The current tower is a replica of a much older structure, which collapsed in 1902.

Rialto Bridge (Ponte di Rialto)
This widely recognized bridge is one of the city's major icons, and dates back 800 years. The first bridge at the site was a wooden structure that collapsed in 1524, while the current bridge was completed in 1591.

La Fenice Theater (Teatro La Fenice)
Although this theater is a 2003 reconstruction, its opulent golden decorations will still impress. Take a walk inside with an audio guide, and learn about the historical structure that burned down in 1996.

Experience

Take a Water Bus, Water Taxi or Gondola
Each of these water transportations down the Grand Canal offers a side of Venice that is not visible from the streets – amazing architecture flank the water, basking in soft seaside sunlight, while a fascinating parage of Venetian watercraft pass you by.

The Vaporetto water buses cost €7, which is not cheap but still more affordable than gondola rides, which will cost about €80 after some haggling with your gondolieres. You might be able to drive the price down more if several of them are chasing after you.

Explore the Maze That Is Venice and Get Lost
Head to the quieter, less touristy Cannaregio or Dorsoduro sestiere, and meander along their winding cobble stone streets, to get to know the authentic Venice. Allow yourself to get lost, and you may just spot a lovely view, framed by the colorful facades of old Venetian buildings, that no guidebook can tell you about. Best of all, you will be able to enjoy it without having to jostle with the crowd.

Regata 'Storica
If you are lucky enough to be in town on the first Sunday of every September, you will be treated to the historic fleet event that displays nearly 100 varieties of Venetian boats from the city's storied past, including large oarships from the Roman Empire and Medieval times, rowing down the Grand Canal. There are several races during the day as well, featuring brightly painted gondolini, which make excellent photo opportunities and even better memories.

Carnival of Venice
One of the most popular carnivals in the world, Venice's annual carnival is especially appreciated for the unusual and elaborate masks worn by its participants.

Island Hopping around Venice
Boat services take you to the islands around Venice. The most famous of which is Murano, which is known for colorful glass, and Burano, famous for lace, as well as its picturesque streets and houses, each painted a different shade of pastel.

Shopping

Being a major tourist destination, Venice has a flourishing souvenir shopping scene. You can find little stores everywhere, stocked with local specialties like Carnival masks, and marbled paper. Prices vary wildly, so be sure to compare before buying, and try to stay away from places like St. Mark's Basilica.

Eat and Drink

Tourism has driven up food prices in Venice, along with lodging and everything else. Steer away from San Marco and other crowded streets. Instead, head to Dorsoduro area on the south side of the city, where locals and students go to eat for cheap. Of course, you may still wish to participate in the quintessential Venetian experience, and dine beside the canal, but be prepared to splurge for it.

As with many Italians, Venetians meet before dinner for happy hour, which is called "bacari" here. Head to an osteria, and sample typical aperitifs like "spritz", which is a cocktail made of Prosecco wine and Aperol or Campari, while munching on small plates of "cicchetti" – Venetian tapas. These might include small triangular sandwiches, bite-sized rolls with cold cuts, fried balls of minced fish or meat, or meat cooked on a spit.

Bellini is a delicious mixture of white peach juice and Prosecco, that ubiquitous Venetian Champagne-like sparkling wine. It was invented right here in Venice, at a place called Harry's Bar.

PIEDMONT REGION

Located in northwestern Italy, bordering France, Piedmont region is famous for its strong red wines, including some of the best the country has to offer – Barolo, Barbaresco, Barbera, Dolcetto, and Moscato D'Asti. You'll find many vineyards on the Langhe hills around Asti and Alba, and on other hills between Alba and Alessandria. Consider taking a wine tour from the city of Turin, or from Milan, into this famous wine country.

The fertile soil of the region is also famed for producing white truffles that have been compared to gold for their cost and delicacy. A meal here would sure to be memorable and worth the splurge!

BOLOGNA

Most foreign visitors will be familiar with spaghetti Bolognese. While the dish is named after Bologna, it is a poor imitation of the gastronomical delights the city has to offer. Well-known among Italians for its incredible cuisine – considered the best even in this country of amazing food – the city of Bologna is relatively unknown to foreigners.

Aside from its cuisine, known as la cucina Bolognese, this historical city of 380,000 inhabitants is also beautiful second only to Venice, with one of the largest and best-preserved historic centers in Italy. Architecture in the city is noted for its rich palette of terracotta reds, burnt oranges, and warm yellows, while its miles of attractive covered walkways, known as "porticos", are among the most intact in all of Europe.

Sights

Sanctuary of Santa Maria della Vita
This church is famous for "The Lamentation", a life-size terracotta group sculpture by Renaissance artist Niccolò Dell'Arca.

Towers of the Asinelli and Garisenda (Torri degli Asinelli e Garisenda)
The most recognizable landmarks of the city, these astonishing towers were built in the 12th century. Today, Torre degli Asinelli, 97.20 meters tall with 498 steps and an incline of 1.3 meters, is open to public, while Torre del Garisenda, 47 meters tall with a lean of 3 meters, is closed to public.

Basilica di Santo Stefano

Also known as the Seven Churches, this basilica consists of seven interconnected religious buildings dating back to 430 AD. Legend has it that Bishop Petronio, now the patron saint of the city, decided to erect a single building divided into seven parts, which represents the seven places where the Passion of the Christ took place. From the piazza on which it is located, the facades of three churches – the Church of the Calvary, the Church of Saint Vitale, and the Church of Agricola – are visible.

Fountain of Neptune (Fontana di Nettuno)
This famous fountain, built in 1563 by Tommaso Laureti of Palermo, was later embellished by Giambologna, and is considered one of Bologna's most important cultural symbols.

Fountain of Neptune

Piazza Maggiore

A large pedestrian square located in the center of the city's old district, Piazza Maggiore is surrounded by the Basilica of San

Petronio, the City Hall, the portico del Banchi, and the Palazzo del Podesta.

Basilica di San Petronio
Many of Bologna's treasures can be found here at the Basilica di San Petronio, such as the sundial by Cassini and Guglielmini, which indicates the exact period of the current year at all times, the "S. Rocco" by Parmigianino, and the glittering Bolognini Chapel. The museum is located through the left nave of the basilica, and holds many attractive bas-reliefs.

St. Luke's Basilica (Santuario di Madonna di San Luca)
This round basilica, built in mid-18th century, offers one of the best panoramic views of the city. Walk along the 666 arches of its unique portico, before heading inside for the famous icon, the Madonna di San Luca.

Experience

Motor Shows and Car Museums
Right before the winter holidays each year, Bologna hosts the Motor Show. You can also visit Ducati, Ferrari, and Lamborghini Museums, for automobile masterpieces from luxury Italian carmakers.

Buy local food
Before flying out, be sure to pick up packaged local food, such as handmade pastas and gorgeous cheeses, far superior to anything you're likely to find back home. There are hundreds of small vendors all around the city. You can also head to the Quadrilatero, an old Medieval food market, framed by Piazza Maggiore, via Rizzoli, via Castiglione, and via Farini, that has been in existence since Roman times.

Cooking Classes
For a fun and practical experience, take a cooking class from some of the best chefs in Italy while you are in Bologna.

Eat

Eating is what you are chiefly in Bologna to do. Generally considered the culinary capital of Italy with its fabulous local produce cooked ingeniously, Bologna is practically incapable of offering a bad meal.

It goes without saying that you should try fresh pasta in the city where many varieties – tortellini, tagliatelle, and lasagna – originated. Trust us, you have not had pasta as they are meant to be until you've tried them here.

Delicious Tortellini

The city is also famous for its cured pork. Mortadella is an enormous Italian sausage made from finely ground pork, at least 15% of which is the delicious hard fat from the neck of the pig. It is flavored with black pepper, myrtle berries, nutmeg, and pistachios.

Culatello, the "king" of Italian cured meat, is made from the prized hind leg of pigs, salted, massaged and carefully cured before air-drying for a minimum of one year. It offers a fine, intense flavor that you cannot miss.

Bologna is located in the Emilia-Romagna region, which as a whole is known for amazing food. You can find many regional specialties, such as Parmigiano Reggiano cheese, balsamic vinegar of Modena, and Parma ham, right here in Bologna as well.

FLORENCE (FIRENZE)

Florence is the capital city of the Tuscany region in Italy, and one of the country's major cultural, artistic, and architectural gems. From the 1300's to the 1500's, it was the most important city in Europe politically, economically, and culturally, eventually fostering the birth of the Italian Renaissance. Florentines were also the inventors of money in the form of the gold florin, Renaissance and neoclassical architecture, and the opera.

The city was also the seat of the all-powerful Medicis, arguably the most important family in European history, having single-handedly taught the European countries how to conduct statecraft. Then there were the art they sponsored and helped flourish. Without them, and indeed without many of the famous Florentine artists – Botticelli, Piero della Francesca, Michelangelo, and of course, Leonardo da Vinci – the walls of some of the world's best museums today might just look very different.

Sights

Santa Maria del Fiore (Duomo di Firenze)

This most iconic of Florentine cathedrals has become synonymous with the city itself. The huge dome designed by Brunelleschi was a celebrated engineering feat of the Renaissance age. You can scale to the top of the dome, which has 464 steps. A statue of the architect can be found in the piazza outside, looking upwards toward his astonishing achievement.

Giotto's Tower

The tower, located next to the Duomo, offers a magnificent panoramic view of Florence and the surrounding areas. There are 414 steps to the top, so take your physical health into consideration before embarking on the climb.

Galleria degli Uffizi

Some of the world's most famous Renaissance paintings and sculptures from antiquity are housed at the Galleria degli Uffizi, including Botticelli's The Birth of Venus and Primavera, and Titian's Venus of Urbino. Avoid long lines by going in the afternoon, a few hours before the museum closes, or pay a bit extra to reserve online for immediate entry: http://www.b-ticket.com/b-ticket/uffizi/default.aspx.

Academia Gallery

Michaelangelo's well-known masterpieces David, and the unfinished Slaves, can both be found at the Academia.

Palazzo Vecchio

The one time city hall and palace of Florence, Palazzo Vecchio is now a museum adorned with fine art. A replica of Michelangelo's David is placed outside, at the statue's original location. There is also a big collection of Renaissance sculptures and paintings. The da Vinci masterpiece, Battaglia di Anghiari, used to be displayed here as well, but is now sadly lost.

Pitti Palace

Pitti was once the residence of the Medici family, and now serves as a museum for the art and treasures they collected. Behind the building, you can find the Boboli gardens with its wonderful walks, and views of the city as well as the countryside to the south.

Ponte Vecchio

Ponte Vecchio

This famous bridge stretching across the Arno is the only Florentine bridge to have survived World War II. Today, it is lined with shops – mostly jewelers, as it was during the days of the Medici.

Michelangelo Square (Piazzale Michelangelo)

Sitting atop a hill, Michelangelo Square offers the best panoramic view of the city. There is also a copy of Michelangelo's David. You may climb the stairs called "Rampe di San Niccoo" in front of the National Library, or take the bus to reach the top.

Experience

Take a Walking Tour of Florence

Learn more about the city's illustrious history as you walk about this compact and exquisite city. Nearly every building boasts of hundreds of years of history, and its own fascinating backstory.

Watch Street Performers in front of the Palazzo Vecchio
In the evenings, street performers set up in front of Palazzo Vecchio, and attract a good crowd. Performances can range from violin duets to people masquerading as sculptures. It's a nice place to take an after-dinner walk.

Eat and Drink

Traditional hearty Tuscan fare, like the enormous Florentine steak, can be readily found in Florence. Also try lampredotto if you dare, a Florentine fast food dish using cow tripe that has a thousand years of history.

Florence also boasts of possibly the best gelato in all of Italy. It is usually freshly made in the bar where you buy it, and you can try many exotic flavors like watermelon, spumante, or garlic! Florentines eat dinner rather late – between 7PM to 9PM – and most gelato places will be closed by then, so consider having dessert first, before dinner.

Mercato Centrale is a large market that sells affordable fresh food on the ground floor, selling everything from fruits and vegetables to cheese and olive oil. The second floor has many cheap food stalls, with some seating in the middle. It's a great place to find affordable food and drinks.

The local liquor of choice is Chianti, which is pretty cheap at many Florentine eateries, with their own "house Chianti".

SIENA

Located just a short train ride from Florence, the Tuscan city of Siena was a wealthy Medieval city-state known today for Il Palio, its world famous horse race conducted twice a year in the summer. The city's contribution to art and architecture is quite unique, and of no less importance than Florence.

During Il Palio

Sights

Siena Cathedral (Siena Duomo)
The stately black and white Siena Cathedral includes the Liberia Piccolomini Baptistery, and an attached Museum dell'Opera del Duomo, where you can see the famous Maesta by Duccio. After you've seen the art, ascend to Il Facciatone in the museum for a panorama of the city.

Piazza del Campo
The piazza at the city center is shell shaped, and twice a year serves as the racetrack for Il Palio.

Mangia Tower (Torre del Mangia)
This 88 meter tall tower, built to the exact height of the Siena Cathedral as a sign that church and state wield equal power in the city of Siena, offers amazing views, but is a bit tough to hike its 300 steps, not to mention claustrophobic, as only 25 people are allowed into the cramped staircase at a time. But once you are at the top, the view will make you forget all of that.

Palazzo Pubblico
This palazzo served as Siena's city hall for almost 800 years, through its proud lineage. The museum now contains the famous frescos on good and bad government by Ambrogio Lorenzetti, frescoes by Simone Martini and Duccio. It is also where you would access the Mangia Tower.

Experience

Il Palio
Siena's famous horse race is about more than just racing horses, strangely. It has a lot to do with the city's neighborhood pride and rivalry, and represents a continuation of traditions of religion, pageantry, trash-talking, bragging, and occasional violence, passed down from Medieval times. Unlike in more touristy cities, Siena is not putting on this race for the tourists' enjoyment – in fact, you may feel least welcomed during the Palio than at any other time. This is a Siennese tradition, one the city treasures.

There are currently 17 contrades participating in the two annual horse races, on July 2 and August 16. All locals are affiliated with one of the teams, and feel such loyalty to their team that puts even an avid football fan to shame. At some point, in addition to horse races, there were also fist fights – something like soccer hooligans getting into trouble with one another – but heavy police presence has put a stop to that particular tradition.

Wine Tours
The entire region of Tuscany is renowned for winemaking. As such, you can book a wine tour into the countryside from many Tuscan cities, including Siena.

Eat

A Siennese classic is panforte, a dense cake made of honey, flour, almonds, candied fruits, and a secret blend of spices. It is only commercially made in Siena and the nearby city of Monteriggioni. The most ubiquitous brand is Sapori, which you can get readily in local supermarkets. But if you can, stop by cafes like Nannini on Banchi di Sopra, where you can have fresh panforte and other regional pastries, and buy some for people back home before you leave!

SAN GIMIGNANO

The quaint town of San Gimignano, surrounded by medieval walls, makes a great day trip if you are Siena or Florence, for its beautiful towers and great art.

Sights

San Gimignano Bell Towers

There are a total of 14 towers standing in the town today, out of the original 72 which were built by the wealthy when the town was sacked by Florence. Many were torn down when the city came under Florentine control.

Torre Grossa is the tallest vantage point in the city at 200 feet. A ticket will get you to the top of the tower for stunning views of the town and surrounding Tuscany vista, and into the Pinacoteca Civica museum.

Piazza del Duomo
The town's main square, presided over by the church of the city, is surrounded by the famous thousand-year-old towers.

Piazza della Cisterna
The focal point of this beautiful piazza is an old stone well that locals used to retrieve water in ancient times. While the well is no longer in use today, the square hosts a market every Thursday, and is home to some of the best restaurants in the town.

San Gimignano 1300 Museum
Located in town center, this museum contains a massive reconstruction of the city of San Gimignano as it was during the 13th and 14th century. Entrance is free, so don't miss this opportunity to learn about the town's architectural and cultural heritage, and that of the surrounding area in Tuscany.

PISA

Most visitors come to Pisa just to see the famous Leaning Tower, but it'd be a huge mistake to miss the rest of the beautiful city!

Sights

Piazza dei Miracoli
The piazza will undoubtedly be your first stop in Pisa. This UNESCO World Heritage site contains the Leaning Tower, as well as most other important attractions in the city.

Leaning Tower of Pisa (Torre Pendente)
We don't need to tell you to come see the Leaning Tower. The famous structure was originally planned as the bell tower for Pisa Cathedral. It started leaning soon after construction began in 1173, due to subsidence of the ground beneath. The tower was closed for a while but a project to keep it from toppling over reached a successful conclusion in 2001, so now you may climb to the top once again.

You'll need to reserve a specific time to climb the tower, which is usually 45 minutes to 2 hours after purchase time, but there are plenty of other sights on the piazza alone to occupy you during that time.

Fun fact: while the Tower of Pisa is the most famous, there are two other leaning towers – the Bell Tower of San Nicola Church, and the Bell Tower of San Michele of Scalzi Church, that also lean due to the marsh soil they are built on.

Leaning Tower of Pisa

Pisa Cathedral (Duomo di Pisa)
The city cathedral of Pisa contains artwork by major artists like
Giambologna and Della Robbia. The beautiful Romanesque
structure with double aisles and a cupola, a huge apse mosaic

63

partially by Cimabue, and a fine pulpit by Giovanni Pisano, is full of surprising delights.

Campo Santo Monumentale (Monumental Cemetery)
Like many Italian cemeteries, this building in Pisa is more of a gallery with its collection of ancient Roman sarcophagi, and splendid medieval frescoes by the "Master of the Triumph of Death".

Battistero (Baptistry)
Climb to the dome of this building, and you'll be treated to a great view of the Leaning Tower. The interior of the Battistero features many sculptured decorations, an Arabic-style pavement, pulpit by Nicola Pisano, and fine octagonal font. The acoustics at this building are ingenious – at regular intervals, the ticket checker will come inside, and shout out a few sounds which when echoed, turn into a few beautiful notes from the most delightful music. If you are not shy, try it yourself by standing by the wall, and sing long notes that reverberate into harmonic chords as the echoes travel round and round in the dome at the top.

Experiences

Luminara Festival
Once a year on June 16th, Pisa pays respect to its patron saint – San Ranieri, with the Luminara festival. At sunset, all lights along the Arno are dimmed, and replaced by more than 10,000 candles. It's a stunning sight from the Ponte di Mezzo. The night is completed by activities on the street, and end with a big firework show.

Spa Day
Casciana Terme has served as a thermal bath since ancient times. Many of the water's healing powers are just in recent years being studied, but no scientific inquiry is necessary to enjoy the relaxing atmosphere after a long day of sightseeing.

MONTEPULCIANO

The Tuscan city of Montepulciano is famous for its classic red wine, Vino Nobile di Montepulciano, considered one of Italy's best, among other well-made libations. It also produces great pork, cheese, "pici" pasta, lentils, and honey. Stop by for a day trip, and enjoy the laid-back hill town while treating yourself to a scrumptious meal.

Sights

Piazza Grande
A beautiful square surrounded by beautiful buildings on all sides, Piazza Grande should not be missed. You'll find the stunning architectural marvels of Palazzo Comunale, Contucci Palace, and Palazzo de' Nobili-Tarugi.

Climb to the top of the clock tower of Palazzo Comunale for a great view of the town, and enjoy a fun wine tasting in the basement of Contucci Palace, where the city's jail has been converted into a cantina.

Experiences

Avignonesi Winery
Situated on the border of Tuscany and Umbria, Avignonesi is a scenic hillside spot for wine tasting that includes a tour of the facilities, culminating in a delicious lunch, paired of course, with the wine produced on site.

ROME

Rome, that ancient capital of the western civilization, the Eternal City, and today the largest city in Italy – no trip to the country is complete without a few days wandering the millennia-old Roman streets, and take in the haphazardly put together charm of 2,800 years of human existence, concentrated in this now sprawling metropolitan.

Rome's historical heritage is incomparable – the entire historic center of the city is a UNESCO World Heritage Site filled with wonderful palaces, churches, ruins, monuments, statues and fountains, all of staggering degrees of age. Outside the old districts, modern Rome offers worldly comforts such as nightlife and shopping. Together, Rome of past and present draw millions of visitors each year, making it one of the world's most visited cities.

Roman Forum

Sights

Ancient Rome

Pantheon

As its name implies, this magnificent temple, dating back to the time of the first emperor of the Roman Empire – Augustus Caesar, was once dedicated to all gods of the Roman state religion. The building was reconstructed in 100's AD by Emperor Hadrian, who added its now widely-recognized dome, a true marvel of ancient architecture.

The Christian Church appropriated the building in the 7th century. It is the only building from the Graeco-Roman world that has remained intact and in continuous use to the present day. Under Christian use, it was formerly known as the Basilica of Santa Maria and Martyrs, and serves as the burial ground for the first two kings of Italy – Vittorio Emanuele II and Umberto I, along with their spouses.

Standing directly beneath the oculus of the majestic dome, you can see traces of the former bronze ceiling, which was melted down during the reign of Pope Urban VIII to make bombards for the fortification of Castel Sant'Angelo.

Piazza Campo de' Fiori

This open piazza, often bathed under the hot Roman sun, is used as a marketplace during the day, while students, lovers, and tourists stroll at night when it is lit by street lamps. You can find a statue of a hooded figure – Giordano Bruno, in the middle. The excommunicated Dominican monk, and one of the earliest cosmologists to have conceived the idea of an infinite universe, was burnt at the stake on this spot in 1600.

If you are lucky, you may catch a young vocalist belting out O Sole Mio at the top of his lungs here. It's a treat!

Piazza Navona

Piazza Navona, established in the 15th century, preserves the shape of the ancient Roman Stadium of the Emperor Domitian. Buildings have replaced the stands where Roman spectators once sat watching chariot races. Today, the square is off-limit to traffic, hence a popular spot to take it slow – sip coffee, shop, and people watch. There are several monuments on the square. Look for the two masterpieces by Baroque artists Bernini and Borromini.

Colosseum

This most famous of Roman landmarks, known once as the Flavian Amphitheater, was originally the site of animal fights and gladiatorial combats capable of supporting some 50,000 spectators. The massive building measures an astonishing 48 meters high, 188 meters in length, and 156 meters in width. The wooden floor where gladiators' blood once spilt is 86 meters by 54 meters, and would have been covered in sand during Roman days.

The line is predictably long here, but you could opt for a tour to bypass the crowd. The knowledgeable archaeologists leading the tours have a wealth of knowledge on anything you might want to know about the amphitheater. Or, you could buy a one day or a three day pass from across the street at the Roman Forum, which allows you to skip the lines as well.

Palantine Hill

This hill was once where the rich and famous of the Romans built their villas. Today you can still see the ruins of several prominent Roman families.

The Roman Forum

This was once the center of Roman life – Senators gathered in the square to make important decisions for the biggest empire in the world, priests gathered here to make sacrifices, and judges to preside over cases of every kind. Located between the Capitoline and Palatine hills, the Forum is still paved by some original stones left from the Roman period. While it is less crowded than the more imposing Colosseum these days, it was in the Forum that most businesses of the empire would have been conducted on a day-to-day basis, all those thousands of years ago.

Modern Rome

Trevi Fountain

This highly recognizable Baroque fountain features a mythological sculptural composition of Neptune, the Roman god of the seas, flanked by two vividly rendered tritons: one struggling to control a violent seahorse, while the other controls a pacified creature, together symbolizing the dual nature of the oceans. Completed in 1762, the location of the fountain actually marks the much older terminus of the Aqua Virgo aqueduct, completed in 19 BC to supply the Baths of Agrippa with running water. It is named for its location on the junction of three roads – tre vie.

The tradition for visiting Trevi Fountain is to throw a coin into the water, so that one may one day return to the city, or, for the more romantic visitor, two coins so that one may fall in love with a beautiful Roman girl (or a handsome Roman boy), while three signify the thrower will marry that Roman in Rome itself. The proper way is to throw the coin using one's right hand, over one's left shoulder. The large amount of coins thrown into the fountain is actually regularly collected to finance charities.

Unfortunately Trevi Fountain is currently under restoration. You will only be able to use a suspended plexiglass walkway to take a closer look, but the restoration process should end within the year.

Via Veneto (Vittorio Veneto)

A popular site featured in Fellini's 1960 film La Dolce Vita, Via Veneto is also the location of the U.S. Embassy in the Palazzo Margherita. There are many roadside cafes to sit and people watch in.

Quirinal Palace (Palazzo del Quirinale)
Originally built in 1583 to serve as a papal summer residence, Quirinal Palace has since served as the residence for the Pope, the King of Italy, and now, the home of the president of the Italian Republic.

North Center

Villa Borghese
The villa contains a garden that is very pleasant to stroll in, Rome's Zoo, a pond where you can rent a rowing boat for a romantic ride, and the Piazza di Siena.

Also situated on the villa grounds is Galleria Borghese, one of the best museums in the world, in the 17th-century villa. In just 20 rooms, you can view treasures from Antiquities, the Renaissance, and the beginnings of the Baroque period. You'll need to reserve tickets ahead of time, but this also means that you won't have to jostle for a good view of Bernini's masterpieces.

Spanish Steps (Scalinata di Spagna)
These 135 steps, confusingly built with French funds to link the Bourbon Spanish embassy to the Holy See in 1721 to 1725, are truly monumental. The climb is absolutely essential to complete a trip to Rome. You'll find tourists and locals alike hanging on these steps.

Spanish Square (Piazza di Spagna)
The most famous square in Rome, Spanish Square was the meeting point of all foreigners visiting the city, and in the 17th century, served as the residence of the Spanish Ambassador to the Holy See. There is a lot to see, including the Fontana della

Barcaccia by Pietro Bernini, father of the more famous sculptor Gian Lorenzo Bernini. The name of the statue means "old boat fountain", celebrating the fact that before high walls were built along the Tiber, Rome was often flooded by rising water so high that once a boat ended up in this very square. The piazza is also home to a column commemorating the Immaculate Conception, and Italy's very first McDonalds, opened in 1986.

Vatican City
The smallest independent state in the world and the seat of the Pope, the Vatican is in a league of its own, though it is entirely surrounded by the city of Italy. Aside from Vatican City, there are also 13 buildings in Rome and one at Castel Gandolfo that enjoy the same independent extraterritorial rights.

St. Peter's Basilica
If Vatican City is the center of the Catholic world, then St. Peter's Basilica is the center of Vatican City. This magnificent basilica is topped by a dome designed by Michelangelo, and is of such an astonishing proportion that pictures could never do it justice. For a frame of reference, the Statue of Liberty, which is 92 meters tall, can fit easily under the dome, which has an interior height of 120 meters, with plenty of room for a helicopter to hover over.

After you take in the interior, take an elevator up to the roof, and then hike up the 323 steps to the very top of the dome for a spectacular view of Rome. This is not an easy climb, but if you are physically fit, this is not the place to be lazy and miss out. There is also a crypt underneath the structure, where you can see the tomb of Pope John Paul II.

Note that as in most places of worship in Europe, you should dress respectfully with your shoulders and most of your legs (so no mini skirts) covered, and men must take off their hats upon entering.

View of St. Peter's Basilica from Trastevere

Seeing the Pope

The head of the Catholic Church is surprisingly accessible. You can either see a usual blessing from his apartment at noon every Sunday – except in the summer when he gives it at this summer residence at Castel Gandolfo), or attend the formal Wednesday appearance, when he arrives at 10:30 to bless crowds from a balcony or platform, or in the Aula Paolo VI auditorium next St. Peter's Square in the winter.

St. Peter's Square

Though called a square, St. Peter's Square is actually an ellipse-shaped space. It contains many fountains designed by two different architects, Carlo Maderno and Gian Lorenzo Bernini. The Obelisk situated in the center was brought back from Egypt by the terrible Emperor Caligula to mark the spin of a circus, which was eventually completed by another terrible emperor, Nero.

The Vatican Museums

As the Church has always sponsored a large quantity of art, the Vatican Museums house one of the greatest art collections in the world. Ascend the spiral staircase to find the Raphael Rooms, and the exquisitely decorated Sistine Chapel with Michelangelo's frescoes. The lines can be long here, so try to book online in advance so you can skip ahead.

Swiss Guard

Their colorful striped uniforms may make them look like they belong in the circus, but these soldiers are charged with the very serious task of protecting the Pope himself. The Pontifical Swiss Guard is the oldest and smallest standing army in the world, having been founded in 1506 by the "Warrior Pope" Julius II, who also spearheaded the construction of the new basilica, and the Sistine Chapel's new paint job by none other than Michelangelo himself.

Experiences

Walking Around in the Old City

The city of Rome is an outdoor museum that can only be taken in by wandering around the old city. Parts of it are still paved with uneven cobblestones, lending a small town charm to this major metropolitan. Look up, and you'll find amazing roof gardens, sculptures, paintings, and religious icons, attached to the exterior walls of the old houses. You can also look through the archway entrances of larger palazzos to see beautiful courtyards complete with sculptures, fountains, and gardens. Just like in ancient Roman days, the area between Piazza Navona and the Tiber is filled with artisans working on a myriad of trades from their small workshops.

Explore Trastevere

Trastevere, a district in Rome that literally means "beyond the Tiber River", is home to lots of restaurants, bars, and small cobbled streets. Unlike much of this touristy city, in Trastevere you can get great Italian food at very reasonable prices. There are also lots of decorated outdoor seating areas that are very romantic. Allow yourself to wander and get lost down the narrow and winding paths here, and you may find charming spots you might not have otherwise found.

Shopping around via del Corso and via Condotti and Surrounding Streets
For high-end shopping in Rome, visit via Condotti and surrounding streets, while via del Corso offers more affordable options. Via Cola di Rienzo is also a good place to browse.

Day Trips to Orvieto or Naples
If you want to get out of Rome for a bit, both Orvieto and Naples are great options. Orvieto is a beautiful little town, while Naples in the south, just an hour away on speed train, shows a slower, more leisurely side of Italy you may not find in busier cities like Milan and Rome.

Eat

For a more authentic culinary experience away from the tourist traps, you'll want to wander out of the historical center, and hit up a real Italian neighborhood where locals live. Trastevere is a great option.

Pizza is of course a must-try here in Rome. The pie of choice here is thin crusted, crunchier, with far less pizza topping compared to the thicker classic Neapolitan pizza. Most restaurants only serve pizza in the evening. You can also get something called pizza al taglio, which has a thicker crust and is served in pieces usually for take away. It is cheap, filling, and fun to eat as you are walking down the street.

On a hot Roman summer, grab some gelato to cool yourself down. You'll find them across the city, and they are really mostly great.

ORVIETO

Orvieto is an ancient Etruscan city, built on top of a steep hill as an impregnable stronghold. The city rises above the dramatic vertical faces of cliffs, surrounded by defensive walls built of the same volcanic stone of the cliff. Just 90 minutes away from Rome, it is a perfect day trip away from the capital.

Sights

Duomo of Orvieto
The main attraction in the town, the Duomo was constructed in the 13th and 14th centuries. It is located on the Orvieto hill, and thus imposingly visible from miles away in the Umbrian countryside. Its black and white striped façade is designed as a mixture of Romanesque and Gothic styles, but the real allure of the cathedral is inside, where you can see the frescoes of Luca Signorelli on the theme of the Last Judgment inside the Capella di San Brizio.

Palazzi Papali
Just behind the Duomo is this collection of medieval palaces, which now house the city's best devotional art. The most important piece is the marble Mary and Child sitting underneath a bronze canopy, attended by exquisite angels. A replica of the ensemble is in the niche in the center of the Duomo's façade, while the real deal is here in the palaces.

Other Sights
There are many other architectural marvels located in this walled city, including the Piazza del Popolo, Saint Patrick's well, La Cava well which dates from the Etruscan time, Corso Cavour which hosts a shop and restaurants, the medieval quarter, Saint Giovenale, Saint Giovanni, and Saint Francesco churches,

Albornoz rock, and the surrounding promenade in the downtown area.

Experience

Underground Tunnels

Hidden beneath the streets is another side to the city – an extensive network connecting secret caves, dug deep into the volcanic rock that forms the earth here. Take a subterranean tour to explore this labyrinth, which has also yielded many archaeological treasures throughout the years.

Drink

Orvieto is known for its "Classico" white wine, made to the northeast of the city.

SOUTHERN ITALY

NAPLES

Located in the south of Italy, in the Campania region, Naples is the third most populated city in the country. The city's history can be traced back to the 7th and 6th century BC, when Greeks established a colony named Neapolis, which means "new city".

Walking through Naples, you'll find the city rather different from other major European cities like, say, Milan – many buildings are a bit rundown and covered in graffiti, and the streets somewhat dirty. But whereas many of those posher European cities start to feel all the same, Naples definitely possesses a unique blend of charm not found anywhere else.

Sights

Sansevero Chapel (Museo Cappella Sansevero)
This dazzling Baroque style chapel, named after the Sangro di Sansevero princes who commissioned it, is both one of the most beautiful structures you'll see in Italy, and a little bit spooky, as it served as the funerary chapel for the princely family, and still contain a few skeletal displays in the crypt, commissioned by the seventh Sangro di Sansevero prince, Raimondo, who modified the building's style to its current Baroque, and laid the splendid marble-inlay floor.

Bourbon Tunnel
Discover your own appetite for adventure down in the Bourbon Tunnel, which had been in turn an aqueduct, an escape route, an air raid shelter, and an impound lot during its 500 years of history. The tunnel descends 30 meters into Monte Echia, and emerges again in Chiaia's Parcheggio Morelli. You can only visit the tunnel by joining a guided tour.

Teatro di San Carlo (Royal Theater of Saint Charles)
Impressively the oldest opera house in all of Europe and one of the oldest continuously active public opera venues in the world, Teatro di San Carlo is one of the Naples' most stunning sights. The theater first began operating in 1773, and still hosts an opera season from late January to May, and a ballet season from April to early June, with a capacity of 3,285.

Lungomare
Between via Partenope and via Francesco Carrociolo along the seafront is the relaxing and quiet pedestrian strip known as Lungomare. Stretching 2.5 kilometers in length, the strip offers an exquisite view of the bay, Mt. Vesuvius, two castles of Vomero's many villas. At dusk, Capri and the distant volcano take on a soft orange hue, adding to the romantic atmosphere of this walk.

Via San Gregorio Armeno

Known as "Christmas Alley", via San Gregorio Armeno is a narrow cobble stoned alley that hosts a number of artisanal workshops that produce the famous Neapolitan nativity scenes and figures, known as "preseni". It is located in Naples' historic distric, Centro Storico, between via dei Tribunali and via San Biagio dei Librai.

Eat

The most famous of Neapolitan cuisine is something we all know and love – pizza! While in Naples, be sure to try pizza margherita, the original with fresh tomatoes, basil, fresh mozzarella, and a little olive oil. None of that meat lover Hawaiian stuff! The pizza here is going to be better than what you've had before, even in Rome or other Italian cities. Almost every pizzeria you come upon will serve a great pie.

Other than pizza, Neapolitan cuisine features a lot of seafood owing to its position on the sea. They will usually be sautéed in garlic, extra virgin olive oil, tomatoes and some kind of local red wine based sauce. Some sauce names like "arrabbiata" (angry" or "fra diavolo (brother devil" imply that it is spicy.

POMPEII

Also in the Bay of Naples is situated the most famous ancient ruin in the world – Pompeii, which was an ancient Roman city overrun by hot lava when nearby Mt. Vesuvius erupted in 79 AD. As everything was frozen in time, Pompeii has been an excellent source for studying the daily lives of ancient Romans – from what was in their pickle jars, to where their prostitutes worked. Nearby Herculaneum suffered much of the same fate. Walk around these ancient towns, and feel the impossibly direct connections you have with people of two thousand years ago.

Sights

The Amphitheatre
Completed in 80 BC, Pompeii's amphitheater predates the Coloseum by nearly 200 years and is th earliest surviving permanent amphitheater located in Italy. In its heyday, it measured 135 meters by 104 meters, and could hold up to 20,000 spectators for the city's holidays and shows.

The Great Palaestra (Gymnasium)
In a large plot of land across the amphitheater is the gymnasium, which was used by the city's young men for sporting events, training, and swimming in the pool in the center. Colonnades surround the grounds on three sides.

Forum
As with the Forum in Rome, here was the center of public life in Pompeii. Before the eruption, this square would have been surrounded by many governmental, religious, and business buildings.

Baths

Several baths in Pompeii were preserved by volcanic ashes. The Forum Baths are well-preserved and roofed. You need to go through a long entranceway before coming inside. The Central Baths are larger but not as preserved, while the Stabian baths are interestingly decorated and present a clearer picture of how baths worked in Roman times.

Villa dei Misteri (Villa of the Mysteries)
Located outside the ancient city walls, the Villa of the Mysteries is covered in curious and finely painted frescos, some of which feature women being initiated into the ancient Greek cult of Dionysus.

CAPRI (ISLAND)

Just 5 kilometers off of the mainland is the Island of Capri, where the suspicious Roman emperor Tiberius built his villa in fear of assassinations (and, as rumor has it, to host debauched orgies). The island is otherwise known for its scenic beauty, and has been a favorite coastal resort of Italians since the Roman times. It was also where the fabled sirens made their home.

Sights

Blue Grotto (Grotta Azzurra)

The most famous attraction in Capri is the Grotto Azzura – the Blue Grotto, which is a sea cave illuminated by an ethereal blue light. Local fishermen have known about the beautiful locale for ages, but it was not until 1826, when two German tourists, writer Augustus Kopisch and painter Ernst Fries, came upon the cave, that it came widely known to outsiders. Subsequent research revealed that Tiberius built a quay in the cave, complete with a nymphaeum, in the grotto. Today, towards the rear of the cave, you can still see the carved Roman landing stage.

The otherworldly blue light for which the grotto is named comes from sunlight entering a small underwater aperture, which is then refracted through the water, and the sunlight reflecting off the white sandy seafloor.

Taking a tour from Marina Grande is the easiest way to visit the grotto. The ticket (€26.50), covers round trip on the boat, a rowing boat into the cave, the cave's admission – as well as the singing captains. So don't feel obliged to give them a tip.

Villa Jovis

This sprawling villa is built directly on a cliff, so as to prevent assassins from entering the house of the paranoid Emperor Tiberius. After visiting the villa, you can visit Church of Santa Maria del Soccorso, the Cave of Tiberius, and the Lighthouse Tower, all close to here.

Experience

Take the Chairlift Ride

The lift takes you up to Monte Solaro in 15 minutes, and pass by some private homes with well-kept gardens and orchards. Stay for a bit looking out over the bay of Naples from the summit.

Walk

Many tourists only take boat trips around the island, but by walking through foot paths (many of which can be steep), you'll get to see beautiful sights like "Arco Naturale" that they do not get to see.

Hike

Around the entire perimeter of the island are hiking trails that offer otherwise inaccessible views both on the island, and out to the sea. You'll find some abandoned forts that make for interesting photo opportunities, and go all the way down to the water. It's a great way to avoid the crowds.

SORRENTO

Charming Sorrento is situated on a long cliff close to Naples, Pompeii, the Amalfi Coast, Mt. Vesuvius, with ferries running to Capri, making it an ideal base to explore all of these locations. Lemon and olive groves fill the town, which overlooks the sea. The old part of the town still retains its Roman grid of narrow streets, and across a ravine, is where the suburban area and hotels are   located.

Sights

Church of San Francesco (Chiostro di San Francesco)

Visit the Church of San Francesco, dating back to the 14th century, for its arches and architecture. There are also a convent and a cloister nearby, both also under Saint Francis.

Piazza Tasso
At the center of life in Sorrento is Piazza Tasso. There are lots of cafes, restaurants, shops, fruit stands, and even horse-drawn carriages that can take you on a tour of the whole town. If you are tired of constant walking and sightseeing, sit a bit and relax here.

Experience

Swim
Sorrento has two swimming spots – Marina Grande, or the better option, Marina Piccola, which is the main beach to the west of the ferry and boat harbor.

Day Trip to Capri
Ferries run regularly from Sorrento to Capri.

Visit the Amalfi Coast
You can take a drive along the scenic Amalfi Drive from Sorrento, to arrive at the beautiful Amalfi Coast, or take a boat ride along the coast if you'd prefer.

Drink

Limoncello di Sorrento
The local liquor of choice, Limoncello is made from lemon rind and quite strong. The related Crema al Limone is similar, but cream-based and less strong.

AMALFI COAST

The Amalfi Coast, located in the southwestern region of Campania, is renowned for its extraordinarily beautiful seascape, and the collection of medieval colorful rustic villages that are built on sloping hills amid thriving lemon groves that lend a fresh scent to the entire region. Every town is uniquely charming, so be sure to drive to a few while you are here.

Amalfi Coast near Positano

Sights

Positano
Possibly the most famous of the Amalfi villages, Positano winds from an enclave on the face of a hill, all the way down to the azure water. It is always full of vacationers, but spring would be the best and least crowded time in general.

Positano

Amalfi
The largest city on the Amalfi Coast, Amalfi is situated on the mouth of a deep gorge, and a very romantic location. The Duomo, dating from the 10th century, has a magnificent tower that is visible from the harbor, while the cloisters next door, built in the 13th century, houses a series of beautiful mosaics and paintings, and 120 columns in the exotic Arabic style.

Amalfi is a good base for day excursions to Capri and the Grotta dello Smeraldo.

Ravello

The enchanting village of Ravello takes you back to a quieter and more peaceful time. Perched high on a ridge above Amalfi, Ravello offers a stunning view of the Mediterranean from a high vantage point.

The architecture of the town is just as impressive. Visit the renowned gardens, the beautiful Villa Rufolo, and the Duomo, located in Vescovado Square. The gem of the bunch, however, is Villa Cimbrone, which has drawn many famous fans over the years, including E.M. Forster, Virginia Woolf, D.H. Lawrence, and Winston Churchill. The beautiful estate is dotted by many replicas of Roman busts, including a statue of the god Mercury. Do not miss the Terrace of Infinity, which is situated above a cliff over the ocean. Gore Vidal, upon visiting the Terrace, said that it offered the most beautiful sight he had ever experienced.

PLANNING YOUR TRIP

BEST TIME TO VISIT ITALY

July and August are when Italy is most crowded and expensive to visit, as many Italians and other Europeans are on vacation, driving prices high and queues at attractions long. The same applies for holidays like Christmas, New Year, and Easter. In addition, December to March is the ski season, and visiting the Alps and the Dolomites can be expensive.

The best times to visit are spring to early summer, or early fall. In general, in April to June, September to October, you should be able to score good deals on accommodation, especially in southern Italy. The weather is less hot and humid as well, making for a more enjoyable experience. In the spring, you'll see beautiful flowers and fresh local produce, as well as a number of festivals. In the autumn, you'll have warm, temperate weather, and grapes would have just been harvested at vineyards across the country.

November to March is low season. While prices will the cheapest, some sights and hotels in coastal and mountainous areas will be closed. This won't be a problem for major cities like Rome and Florence, however.

EXCHANGE RATES

Unit = Euro (€)

Rates are calculated at the time of this writing. Please check before your departure for the up-to-date exchange rate.

USD: 1 Dollar = 0.9 Euro
Canadian Dollar: 1 Dollar = 9.71 Euro

British Pounds: 1 Pound = 1.39 Euro
Australian Dollar: 1 Dollar = 0.67 Euro

Visa Information

Italy is a member of the Schengen agreement. There are no border controls between countries that have signed the treaty, so citizens from those countries can freely cross into Italy. Many non-EU countries are visa-exempt. Citizens from those countries will only need to produce a valid passport when entering the country, as the stamp counts as a declaration. For more information, visit the Italian Ministry of Foreign Affairs website: http://www.esteri.it/mae/en/ministero/servizi/stranieri/default.htm l.

US: eligible for visa-free stay, up to 90 days
Canada: eligible for visa-free stay, up to 90 days
Australia: eligible for visa-free stay, up to 90 days

ESSENTIAL ITALIAN CULTURE TO KNOW

Italians are in general very patriotic, though people from different regions are proud of their regional heritage as well. They are also more often than not open and friendly, and enjoy interacting with people of every kind. Paying compliments is generally a good way to make friends. For example, tell someone how beautiful his or her town is will work wonders, especially if you can compare their town favorably to another city.

Don't be shy about asking the locals for restaurant recommendations! Italy is filled with good food, and it would be a crime to eat at tourist traps instead of sampling authentic local cuisine. Very often, the locals can point you to their favorite spots off the beaten path, which will be cheaper and more tasty than what you can find on your own in the touristy areas.

Theft is a common problem, especially in large cities like Naples and Rome. Rome is full of pickpocket, though violent crimes are rare. In public areas, crowded metros and buses, hold onto your handbags and wallets. Men should avoid putting their wallets in their back pockets. You should also watch out for gypsies.

USEFUL ITALIAN TERMS AND PHRASES

In larger cities, you'll likely find someone who speaks English, but in a small town or less touristy areas, it'll be helpful to have some Italian phrases.

Do you speak English: Parla Inglese?

Thank You: Grazie.

You are welcome: Prego.

Please: Per favore; Per Piacere.

Good Morning/Good Afternoon: Buon Giorno.

Good Evening: Buona Sera.

Good Night: Buona note.

How are you (singular): Come sta?

How are you (plural): Come state?

Excuse me: Mi scusi/Scusi.

Hello/Goodbye: Ciao.

How much does it cost: Quanto costa?

Where is ...: Dov'è ....?

Lavatory/Toilet: Gabinetto/Bagno.

To eat: Mangiare

Where is the ... Embassy: Dove si trova... l'ambasciata?

Restaurant: Ristorante.

Stamp: Francobollo.

Postcard: Cartolina.

May I take photos: Posso fare fotografie?

Where can I find a...: Dove posso trovare un.../

I have a booking/we have a booking: Ho una prenotazione/Abbiamo una prenotazione.

Would like something to eat: Vorrei qualcosa da mangiare.

I would like something to drink: Vorrei qualcosa da bere.

How can I go to...: Come posso andare a...

I am allergic to...: Sono allergico a...

Do you accept credit cards: Accettate carte di credito?

Prescription: Prescrizione/Ricetta.

May I pay at check-out: Posso pagare al check-out?

Check please: Il conto, per favore.

Is there internet connection: C'è la connessione ad internet.

How much does it cost? / How much does this cost: Quanto costa? / Quanto costa questo?

Police: Polizia/Carabinieri.

Taxi: Taxi.

Bus stop: Fermata dell'autobus.

Airport: Aeroporto.

Train station: Stazione.

Pharmacy: Farmacia.

Doctor: Medico.

Hotel: Albergo/Hotel.

Pain: Dolore.

Blisters: Vesciche.

Food store: Supermercato.

Shop: Negozio.

Hospital: Ospedale.

Emergency room: Pronto soccorso.

Museum: Museo.

Ticket desk: Biglietteria.

Guidebook: Guida turistica.

Guided tour: Visita guidata.

Opening time: Orario di aperture.

Go away: Vai via!

CONCLUSION

We hope this pocket guide helps you navigate Italy and find the most memorable and authentic things to do, see, and eat.

Thank you for purchasing our pocket guide. After you've read this guide, we'd really appreciate your honest book review!

Sincerely,
The Wanderlust Pocket Guides Team

Planning a Trip or Seeking Travel Inspiration?

Check out our other Wanderlust Pocket Guides on Amazon
Also available are our comprehensive day-to-day City Guides

CREDITS

Cover design by Wanderlust Pocket Guide Design Team

COPYRIGHT AND DISCLAIMER

Copyright © 2015 by Wanderlust Pocket Guides
Cover illustration © 2015 Wanderlust Pocket Guides Design Team

All Rights Reserved. No part of this publication may be reproduced, stored in a retrieval system, or transmitted in any form or by any means, electronic, mechanical, recording, or otherwise, without the prior written consent of the author.

This book is designed to provide engaging information for our readers. The author is not offering any professional travel planning service or travel consulting. While best efforts have been used in providing accurate, up-to-date information, the author makes no warranty about the completeness or accuracy of its content and is not responsibly for loss, injury, bodily or mental discomfort, or inconvenience sustained by any person using this book.

29758657R00059

Made in the USA
San Bernardino, CA
27 January 2016